BRI REECE

Sacred Not Separate

How Religion and Spirituality Intersect in Modern Life

First published by In59Seconds Publishing Co 2026

First edition

This book was professionally typeset on Reedsy.
Find out more at reedsy.com

To my grandmother Ella Mae Fisher Fair (RIP)
who taught me honor and reverence for God.
To every traveler, seeker, believer, doubter, and devotee
who has ever stood in a sacred space and felt something bigger than themselves.
And to the One Divine Source, who I choose to call God,
that has always been present
in my life. Loving, Guiding and Protecting me
-Bri Reece

Contents

Introduction

Sacred Does Not Mean Separate

There was a time in my life when faith felt very defined, very contained, almost like it had a clear address and a predictable sound. It lived inside a church building with wooden pews and stained glass windows. It sounded like an organ warming up before service and a choir finding its harmony. It looked like my grandmother bowing her head before a meal and closing her eyes with a seriousness that told me she was not playing about God, this was not a performance. God, in my childhood, had structure and felt safe. There were right ways to pray and right ways to worship. There where things you could and could not wear to church. There were scriptures we had to memorize, like the B-Attitudes and the Lords Prayer and weekly services to attend. I never questioned that foundation because it was given to me with love. Honestly I will always be grateful for being raised in the church, it gave me a solid foundation and taught me to believe in something greater than myself.

I was raised in a Christian church called Ephesians Church of God in Christ in Compton California. I say that with pride, not resistance. I enjoyed going to Church. It was a part of my life from the very beginning. It was all I knew, and during those early years in the 1970s, it was not something that felt harsh or overwhelming. The people were kind, they had Sunday school and other cool programs for the kids. The environment felt loving, and there was a sense of community that made it feel safe. The only time it ever felt frightening was when we were taught about hell, and even then, what stayed with me most was not fear, but the faith I saw lived out in the people closest to me.

My grandmother's faith was stable and unshakable. Doctors once told her that she would not live past her forties because of heart disease, yet she lived well into her eighties. She did not spend time arguing about God or trying to convince others of what she believed. Instead, she lived in alignment with her faith every single day, and her belief was strong enough to carry her through raising her baby granddaughters and whatever else life placed in front of her.

I watched her pray through difficult seasons without becoming bitter or losing her sense of peace. I remember hearing her sing hymns on Sunday mornings, worshiping with a sincerity that did not depend on whether life was easy or not. There was something powerful in the way she remained consistent. Her faith was not just something she practiced when things were going well, but something she held onto even when life was hard.

My father, Jesse Paul Fisher, struggled with alcoholism, and I saw my grandmother pray deeply for him. He lost his battle with alcohol related illnesses in 1979. When he passed away, I was only ten years old. She had to bury her youngest child, her baby boy, and somehow find the strength to continue. After his passing, she continued raising his two daughters, my older sister Mary and me, and she did it with love, patience, and unwavering faith.

Her faith was never something she limited to Sundays, even though we were in church far more than just one day a week. We were there on Wednesdays and Friday evenings too, and it was not just routine, it was a way of life. What made her so special was not how often she went to church, but how deeply she lived what she believed every single day.

My grandmother was a strong Texan woman whose faith showed up in everything she did. It was in the way she loved people, in the way she forgave without holding on to bitterness, and in the way she endured life's hardest moments without losing herself. Watching her taught me that faith is not about what you say out of your mouth, but about how you carry yourself, how you treat others, and how you remain faithful and grounded when life tests you in ways you never expected.

At fifty-six years old, I can honestly say that I am still reaping the benefits of her influence in my life. Everything good in me, everything stable in me, and everything rooted in love and strength traces back to her. She taught me how to pray. She instill in me morals and values. She showed me what it looks like to stand strong without becoming hard, and to stay soft without becoming weak.

Those ten years I spent with her shaped me in ways that I am still discovering. The impact she left on my life did not fade over time. It grew with me and carried me through seasons where I needed guidance, even when she was no longer physically here. Her presence, her lessons, and her love became a part of who I am, and that is something I will carry for the rest of my life.

As I grew older and began traveling outside of the environment I had always known, I encountered something that I was not prepared for. I saw people honoring God in ways that did not resemble the services of my upbringing. In Indonesia, I watched devotion expressed through movements and rituals that were unfamiliar to me, yet the sincerity in people's eyes looked exactly like what I had seen in my grandmother's. In Egypt, I walked through sacred spaces that held centuries of prayer and felt a reverence that did not require translation. In Meteora, in Delphi, Greece, I stepped into monasteries suspended between earth and sky and realized that silence itself could feel like worship.

The more I traveled, the harder it became to believe that God only spoke one language. Over time, I began to understand that culture may shape how people express their faith, but it does not limit the presence of God. I came to see that the way a person is raised often influences how they honor the Divine Source, and that difference is not something to judge, but something we should all respect.

In other countries, the buildings looked different. The music sounded different. The way people prayed and carried themselves in worship was not the same as what I had grown up with. Even the rituals and expressions of reverence had changed. Yet through all of those differences, one thing remained constant. The presence I felt was the same. There was still a sense of stillness, humility, and a deep longing for connection that did not depend on language, location, or tradition.

That realization did not pull me away from my Christian foundation. It strengthened it. It allowed me to see my beliefs as part of something much greater, something that extends beyond one way of expression and connects people across cultures in a shared desire for faith, peace, and understanding.

Somewhere along the way, society began drawing a sharp line between religion and spirituality, as if they were opposing forces that could not coexist within the same heart. What once felt like a natural connection to something greater slowly became divided into categories, forcing people to choose sides instead of allowing them to grow. For many of us, that division did not feel right, yet the pressure to conform was very real.

Everywhere I went, I heard people say, “I’m spiritual, not religious,” almost as if they had to defend their position before even explaining it. If you identified as religious, you were often labeled as rigid, overly traditional, or even blind. At the same time, if you leaned into spirituality, especially in a way that stepped outside of what you were taught, you could be misunderstood, judged, or even rejected by the very people who once stood beside you in faith. Some were called lost. Others were labeled as something they were not at all. Words like witch or atheist were thrown around carelessly, as if seeking a deeper understanding of the divine somehow meant you had abandoned God in some way.

That experience can be isolating. It can make you question yourself, make you wonder if you are doing something wrong simply because your heart is searching for something more meaningful, more personal, and more connected. You may find yourself caught between two worlds, not fully accepted by either, while still knowing deep within that your desire to grow spiritually is coming from a genuine place.

The conversation around this has become defensive, driven more by ego than understanding, with both sides quick to dismiss one another instead of keeping an open mind and simply listening without judgment. There is a strong desire for validation, for one path to be seen as the only correct way, and in that ego fueled need to be right, something important has been lost.

What saddened me most was realizing how quickly we forgot that both paths are rooted in the same human desire to connect with something greater than ourselves.

This book is not an attempt to blur distinctions for the sake of comfort, nor is it an attempt to dismantle tradition. It is an invitation to look deeper. It's a gentle challenge to question whether the division we defend so fiercely is actually necessary.

When I reflect on my own life, I can clearly see a thread that runs through every sacred experience I have had, whether it took place inside a church sanctuary or beneath an open sky in another country. Whether I was singing at a gospel concert or standing on top of a mountain in Machu Picchu, Peru, taking in the stillness and allowing myself to be fully present, that same thread remained.

That thread has always been love. Love for the Creator of us all. Love for humanity. It is a love that humbles you rather than inflates you, a love that reminds you that God is not confined to one place, one practice, or one way of being, but can be felt anywhere your heart is open enough to receive it.

The more honest I became with myself, the more I realized that many of the arguments people have about religion versus spirituality are less about God and more about their identity. We attach ourselves to labels because they make us feel secure. But the divine does not need our insecurity to be validated. The source that created all of us is not diminished by cultural differences or personal practices. If anything, the diversity of devotion across the world speaks to the vastness of that Omnipotent source.

When I say sacred is not separate, I mean that the divine is not divided the way we divide ourselves. The sacred is present wherever there is sincerity, humility, and love. It is present in hymns and in silence. It is present in prayer and in meditation. It is present in scripture and in stillness. It is present in community worship and in private meditation. The form may vary, but the essence remains consistent.

My hope in writing this book is simple. I want people to feel less defensive and more open. I want families to sit at the same table without turning belief into a battlefield. I want the person who loves Jesus and also practices meditation to feel whole instead of conflicted. It is my desire that the person who grounds themselves in nature and also respects scripture to feel seen instead of judged. Most of all, I want us to remember that if we truly believe we were created by one divine source, then we are already connected at a level deeper than any label.

What follows is not a debate. It is a bridge. It is an exploration of how different practices can coexist without canceling each other out. It is a reminder that reverence does not require rivalry. If we allow ourselves to approach this conversation with humility rather than ego, we may discover that what we have been separating for years was never meant to be separate at all.

1

The Illusion of Division

When I look at some of the images throughout this book, I do not see opposition. In the image at the end of this particular chapter I see two human attempts to reach for the same presence. On one side stands a cross illuminated by warm light, heavy with history and sacrifice and centuries of devotion. On the other side sits a woman in meditation, her body aligned and still, colors radiating along her spine to symbolize inner balance and awareness. For some people, those two images feel like they belong in completely different worlds. One feels institutional and traditional. The other feels personal and expansive. But the longer I have lived and the more I have traveled, the harder it has become for me to pretend that they are disconnected from one another.

I was raised in a church where reverence mattered. Sentences began with "Giving Honor to God". My grandmother did not treat God casually she taught us to pray her way. Our worship was intentional. The wonderful, moving music, the preaching, the laying of hands, the quiet moments at the altar call, all of it carried weight and meant something to all involved. I learned early that faith was something you respected. It was not a hobby or a trend. It was sacred to people. That foundation shaped me in ways I will never dismiss, and I refuse to speak about it with anything but gratitude because it gave me discipline, a moral foundation, and a deep understanding that there is something greater than myself guiding this life.

What I did not understand as a child was that devotion does not only live inside the walls of the church I grew up in. That realization came slowly as I grew up and step slight out of the box. It came when I stood in countries far from home and watched people bow, chant, kneel, light candles, or sit in stillness with a sincerity that looked remarkably familiar. In Indonesia, I saw reverence expressed differently than in christian church, but the posture of humility felt the same. In Egypt, I walked through sacred temples that had been standing long before my grandmother was born, and the air itself felt rich with prayer and ancestral power. In Meteora, in Delphi, Greece, I stepped into monasteries carved into stone and felt silence become a language of its own. None of those experiences weakened my Christian foundation. Instead, they widened it. They made me realize that the divine does not belong to one culture, one tradition, or one method of access. It is about adopting the practices and belief that resonate with you and allow you to live life to the fullest.

The division we see today between religion and spirituality has become much louder than it needs to be. At its core, it feels like an unnecessary distraction that keeps people separated instead of allowing us to grow together. The truth is simple, and it has always been there. It is done unto you as you believe. That alone should create space for people to walk their own path without judgment, yet somehow we have made it complicated.

I often hear people say with certainty that they are spiritual but not religious, as if religion automatically means rigidity, judgment, or being blindly controlled by the masses. At the same time, I hear others defend religion by dismissing spirituality altogether, calling it misguided or even something negative and dark that should be avoided. Both sides speak with conviction, but somewhere in between those positions, something meaningful gets lost.

What we forget is that both religion and spirituality come from the same place within us. Every human being carries a natural desire to connect with something greater than themselves. Religion created structure around that desire, offering practices and traditions that people hold close to their hearts. Communion is a perfect example, where eating crackers and drinking wine represents something sacred and deeply meaningful to those who believe. That ritual is not questioned or labeled as something negative because it is understood within that framework. But it is indeed a ritual in remembrance of Christ.

Spirituality has its own forms of expression as well, whether that is burning sage to cleanse a space, embracing healing crystals , meditating in stillness, or simply sitting quietly and focusing your thoughts and intentions. In many ways, that stillness feels no different than prayer to me. It is a moment of connection and surrender, a moment of reaching for something beyond yourself. Neither path created the desire for God, for love, or for connection. That desire already exists within all of us.

When people argue about which path is right, there is often something deeper beneath the surface. Fear tends to be at the root of it. There is a fear of being wrong, a fear of losing identity, and a strong fear that if someone else finds peace in a different way, it somehow takes away from their own belief system. Ego can quietly turn devotion into something competitive, when in reality there should be no competition at all. None of us truly knows what comes next after this life, and that alone should create humility instead of division.

There is nothing wrong with allowing people to embrace what brings them peace and happiness, what helps them feel connected to God, and what allows them to move through life with love and clarity. Saying that one way is right and another is wrong creates unnecessary separation, and it can make people feel as though appreciating another perspective means betraying their own. That simply is not true. If God is truly infinite, then that presence cannot be threatened by different expressions of reverence. God's existence is not uncertain or fragile. It does not need to be protected by exclusivity. It exists fully, freely, and without limitation, no matter what.

When I think about it in the simplest terms, I compare it to the sun and the moon. No matter where you are in the world, no matter what you believe, and no matter what name you choose to call the divine, the sun still rises and the moon still takes its place in the night sky. A Buddhist sees it. A Christian sees it. A Hindu sees it. A monk sitting in silence sees it. A mother standing in her kitchen window sees it. Whether you are in China, New Mexico, or anywhere else on this earth, you are looking up at the same amazing sky, one that none of us created and none of us can control.

That realization made things very clear for me. There is

a higher power, a divine source that exists beyond human opinion, beyond labels, and beyond the need for agreement. I choose to call that source God, because that is what feels true and natural to me. At the same time, I no longer feel the need for everyone around me to use the same word in order for it to be valid. I have come to understand that the name a person uses often reflects their upbringing, their culture, and the personal journey they have taken to connect with something greater than themselves.

Some people say God. Others say Yahweh or Elohim. Some speak of Allah. There are those who refer to the Divine as the Universe, Source, or Creator. In certain spiritual communities, names like Ra are used, while others simply choose silence and connection without needing a name at all. When you step back and look at it with an open heart, it becomes clear that people across the world have always been reaching for the same presence and unseen source, even if they call it by different names.

None of those expressions make one person closer to God than another. None of those paths cancel each other out. They simply reflect the many ways human beings have tried to understand something that is far greater than any one definition. When I truly allowed myself to see that, something inside of me softened. The need to correct people, to convince them, or to defend my own beliefs began to fall away.

There is a peace that comes with allowing others to experience their relationship with the Divine in a way that feels real to them. It creates space for connection instead of division. It allows love to exist without conditions. It reminds us that we are not here to control each other's spiritual paths, but to walk our own with sincerity and respect for the journeys of others.

That understanding did not come from being told what to believe. It came from living, from observing, and from growing into a place where I no longer felt the need to force my beliefs onto anyone else. It came from realizing that the existence of a higher power is truth, and truth does not need to be pushed, and that something as powerful as God does not require agreement in order to exist.

There was a time when I thought people had to believe exactly what I believed in order for it to be right. That way of thinking came from a place of ego, even if it was disguised as conviction. Growth allowed me to release that. It allowed me to see that truth does not require force, and that something as powerful as God does not need to be defended through division.

I have learned to keep it simple. If a belief system leads someone to be kind, to be loving, to help others, and to move through the world with compassion and integrity, then that is the presence of God operating through them. That is the energy of something greater expressing itself in a way that uplifts not only the individual, but the people around them as well.

At the same time, if a belief system leads to harm, to judgment, to cruelty, or to actions that bring negativity into the world, then that is not aligned with God. God is not confusion. God is not division. God is not here to make us smaller, harder, or more disconnected from one another. God is here to guide us toward growth, toward love, and toward becoming better human beings.

Just like the sun and the moon, that truth exists whether we choose to acknowledge it or not. It does not require our belief to be real. It simply is.

This book is not an attempt to blur distinctions for the sake of personal comfort, nor is it an attempt to dismantle tradition.

It is an invitation to look deeper. It is a gentle challenge to question whether the division we defend so fiercely is actually necessary.

When I reflect on my own life, I can clearly see a thread that runs through every sacred experience I have had, whether it took place inside a church sanctuary or beneath an open sky in another country. Whether I was singing at a gospel concert or standing on top of a mountain in Machu Picchu, Peru, taking in the stillness and allowing myself to be fully present, that same thread remained.

That thread has always been love. Love for the Creator of us all. Love for humanity. It is a love that humbles you rather than inflates you, a love that reminds you that God is not confined to one place, one practice, or one way of being. God can be felt anywhere your heart is open enough to receive it.

The more I observe different practices, the more I notice the similarities instead of the differences. Whether someone kneels at an altar or sits cross legged on the ground, they are making space to connect with the invisible Divine Source . Whether someone sings gospel music with a choir or listens to the resonance of a sound bowl, they are inviting themselves into peace and spiritual alignment. Whether someone reads scripture or studies energy centers in the body, they are searching for clarity, healing, and meaning. The tools may vary. The intention does not, and intention is what reveals the true heart.

I have come to believe something very simple. If a practice moves a person toward kindness, humility, compassion, self control, and love, then it reflects something divine. If it pushes a person toward cruelty, arrogance, harm, or superiority, then it has drifted away from that source. The measure is not whether it looks familiar to me. The measure is whether it produces love. It truly is that simple. We complicate it because we are human and we attach identity to our methods. But at the center of it all, the standard remains unchanged.

There is only one source of life. People may call that source by different names, and those names carry cultural history and emotional meaning, but the presence itself does not multiply just because the language does. Water remains water regardless of what word you use to describe it. In the same way, the divine remains the divine regardless of whether someone says God, Jehovah, Elohim, Allah, Ra, Universe, or Creator. When I stopped focusing on terminology and started paying attention to my personal transformation, it became impossible for me to pretend that these paths had nothing to do with one another. I found many correlations within them all.

This book is not an invitation to abandon your tradition. It is not a call to dilute your faith or blend everything into something unrecognizable. It is an invitation to humility and acceptance. It is a reminder that sacred does not mean exclusive or separate. Sacred means worthy of reverence and deserving of respect. When we understand that, we no longer feel threatened by someone else's way of connecting with God. We can sit at the same table, attend the same family gathering, and allow each person to honor the divine in the way that speaks to their spirit without turning it into an argument.

At the end of the day, the woman meditating and the cross standing in golden light are not symbols of conflict. They are symbols of humanity reaching upward and inward at the same time. One may be rooted in centuries of tradition. The other may feel more fluid and individualized. But both are responding to the same call that has echoed through human history since the beginning of time: the desire to know where we come from, to understand why we are here, and to feel connected to the source that created us all.

Sacred does not mean ***Separate***. It means we are all participating in some personal practice that makes us feel happy and hopeful, even when our practices, rituals, prayers etc look different it does not make them wrong. When we can truly grasp that, the illusion of division begins to dissolve, and what remains is something much more powerful than argument. Love

2

The Language of the Divine

When you look at the image at the end of this chapter, it is easy to focus on what separates the two scenes. One side feels earthy and quiet, almost intimate in its stillness. A woman sits with sound bowls resting in front of her, crystals arranged nearby, candlelight flickering softly as if the air itself has slowed down to listen. On the other side, there is movement. Water pours over a woman's head as she stands in a river, eyes closed, hands resting over her heart while someone gently supports her through baptism. There is sunlight breaking through the trees, illuminating the moment with something that feels both sacred and deeply personal. Both are beautiful.

If you only look at the surface, you might say these two practices belong to entirely different spiritual worlds. But if you look closely at the pictures of the women in both scenes, you will notice something more important than the tools in their hands. You will see surrender and peace. You will see vulnerability.

You will see a human being stepping into something larger than themselves and allowing it to transform them.

The divine has always spoken in many different languages. Some languages are structured and passed down through generations. Others are intuitive and discovered through personal exploration. Religion developed rituals to give that language clarity and continuity. Spirituality developed practices to make that language experiential and embodied. Neither one invented the desire to know God personally. They simply gave people different ways to participate in it.

When someone is baptized, they are entering water as a symbol of renewal. Water becomes a physical representation of washing away an old identity and stepping into something redeemed. It is not simply about getting wet. It is about believing and declaring, both inwardly and outwardly, that you are choosing alignment with God. There is humility in that moment. There is trust. There is a willingness to surrender control and allow yourself to be carried, even briefly, by something that represents divine cleansing and rebirth.

At the center of it all is belief. That is the key. "According to your faith be it unto you." Matthew 9:29. What you believe shapes what you experience. The person being baptized believes deeply that God is washing away their sins. Someone burning sage believes just as strongly that they are clearing negative energy from their space. When you step back and look at both, the common thread is not the ritual itself, but the faith behind it.

I cannot say that I fully understand why human beings lean so heavily on symbolism, yet I have come to accept that we all do in some way. There is something about engaging in a physical act that helps anchor what we believe internally. Even though I personally believe that many of these intentions can be accomplished without the ritual itself, I understand why those rituals exist. They help us stay focused. They help us return to a state of mind that supports what we are trying to feel, believe, and maintain.

You can speak peace over your life with your own words. You can pray over yourself and your family anywhere, whether you are sitting in your car, standing in your kitchen, or walking outside under the open sky. There is no single location that makes your connection to God more valid than another, because that connection is not tied to a building. It travels with you. It lives within you.

At the same time, there is nothing wrong with using spaces and practices as tools to support that connection. Walking into a church can help shift your mindset, not because God is confined to that space, but because you are stepping into an environment designed to help you focus, reflect, and feel uplifted. Sitting in a meditation class or attending a sound bath can do the same thing. Being surrounded by others who are seeking peace and alignment can strengthen your own ability to remain in that space.

I love the energy I feel when I attend church. There is a warmth, a sense of connection, and a reminder of something greater than myself. I also feel that same sense of peace when I sit with my sound bowls and allow the vibration to move through me. The experience may look different on the outside, but what I am reaching for on the inside is the same.

God is with us always. The energy of God does not come and go depending on where you are in the world. It does not require a building, a specific practice, or a particular setting to exist. It is constant and always present. It lives within you.

What we often seek through rituals and environments is not the presence of God itself, but a way to quiet our minds long enough to feel it.

When someone strikes a sound bowl and closes their eyes, they are also entering into renewal, even though the symbolism looks different. The vibration is intentional and equally as powerful. The sound lingers and moves through the body, creating stillness in a way that words sometimes cannot. In that moment, they are choosing to slow down, to listen, and to realign themselves internally. They are deciding that the noise of the world does not get to control their spirit. They are creating space for peace, for clarity, and for harmony within themselves.

At the end of the day, even though the tools people use may look different, the environments may change, and the rituals may not be the same, the intention behind all of it is still very much alike. People are simply trying to feel connected. They are trying to find peace within themselves and hold on to something that feels steady in a world that can often feel overwhelming. No matter how it looks on the outside, the heart of it is the same desire to feel grounded, whole, and at ease.

When you think about it in simple terms, whether it is water or sound, whether it is cleansing or vibration, both are ways that people try to bring themselves back into alignment with God. One person may step into a baptism pool because that is what they were taught, what they believe in, and what feels right to their spirit. Another person may sit in a quiet space, listening to sound frequencies or focusing on their breath, because that is what helps them reconnect. The methods may look completely different, but the purpose behind them is not.

There is something deeply humbling about allowing yourself

to be seen in those moments. Standing in front of others and being baptized requires a level of vulnerability, a willingness to say that you are ready for change and ready to let go of what no longer serves you. Sitting quietly with yourself, whether in meditation or reflection, asks for that same honesty. It requires you to slow down, to be still, and to admit that your mind and your spirit need attention, care, and realignment.

As I began to notice these similarities, the way I listened to people started to change. I no longer focused on whether their beliefs looked like mine or sounded like what I had been taught growing up. What began to matter more was what their beliefs were producing in their lives. I found myself paying attention to how they treated others, how they handled difficult situations, and how they showed up in the world.

I started asking different questions. I wanted to know if their practices were making them happy and more patient, more compassionate and loving, and more aware of themselves. I paid attention to whether they were learning how to forgive, how to grow, and how to heal from their past. Those things became far more important than the specific words they used or the traditions they followed, because at the end of the day, the real evidence of connection to something greater is reflected in how you live, not just in what you say you believe.

It is easy to get distracted by terminology. Words like salvation, rebirth, awakening, alignment, redemption, frequency, and surrender can start to feel like markers that divide communities. But beneath those words are universal experiences. Every human being knows what it feels like to want a fresh start. Every human being knows what it feels like to long for peace in their own mind. Every human being has moments where they recognize that they cannot carry the weight of life alone.

Religion offers language for those moments. Spirituality offers language for those moments as well. The languages differ, but the ache or desire for God is the same.

What often causes conflict is the assumption that if someone chooses one language, they must be rejecting the other. But that assumption is rarely true. Many people move fluidly between practices without feeling internal conflict until someone else tells them they should. A person can cherish baptism as a sacred declaration of faith and still find value in meditation as a tool for quieting their thoughts. A person can respect the symbolism of water as cleansing and also respect the symbolism of vibration as alignment.

The problem is not the practices themselves. The problem is the insistence that only one method is valid. That insistence usually stems from fear rather than faith. It comes from the belief that truth is fragile and must be defended aggressively. But truth does not collapse simply because someone else approaches it differently. God is and will always be truth, no matter which way you choose to honor him.

When I think about the woman being baptized in this image, I see someone choosing transformation. When I think about the woman striking the sound bowl, I also see someone choosing transformation. Neither woman is mocking the other. Neither woman is claiming superiority. They are both engaged in sacred moments that mean something deeply personal to them.

Perhaps that is what we forget when debates become loud. Behind every ritual is a person that needs that symbolism to strengthen their belief. And That's ok. . Behind every practice is a story. Behind every symbol is a heart that is searching for the ultimate love.

If we could learn to see the humanity behind the method, the conversation would soften. We would realize that water and sound, prayer and meditation, scripture and stillness are all attempts to respond to the same invitation. The invitation is to return to our original true nature, which is love. To be humble and deepen our connection with the divine source that created us.

The divine is not confined to a single tool or spiritual practice. It is not limited by geography, language, or posture. It meets people exactly where they are, in the quiet spaces they are willing to open within themselves. Sometimes that openness looks like stepping into a river, surrounded by witnesses, choosing to be seen in a moment of surrender. Other times it looks like sitting alone in stillness, listening to the soft hum of a sound bowl, allowing that vibration to gently settle the noise within. In both moments, something sacred is taking place, not because of the method, but because the heart has chosen to engage.

When that truth begins to settle into your spirit, something shifts in a way that is hard to explain but impossible to ignore. The question is no longer about which path is right or which practice holds more power. The focus becomes much more personal, much more honest. You begin to ask yourself whether what you are doing is producing love in your life. You start to notice whether you are becoming more patient with others, more compassionate in your responses, and more gentle with yourself. You begin to feel whether your connection to the divine is softening you instead of hardening you.

That is where the intersection truly lives. Not in labels. Not in arguments. Not in the need to prove anything to anyone. It lives in the space where religion and spirituality meet inside the human heart, where structure and freedom come together to guide you toward something deeper. It lives in the quiet understanding that your journey does not have to look like anyone else's in order to be real, valid, and meaningful. That is what *How Religion and Spirituality Intersect in Modern Life* truly reveals, not a conflict, but a connection that has always been there waiting to be seen.

There is, in my heart, one ultimate goal for humanity, and it is not division and competition. It is not proving who is right and who is wrong. It is for each of us to become the greatest version of ourselves, to develop a kind of self love that is so consistent and so authentic that it naturally pours out into the way we treat ourselves and others. We will be able to look at another human being, no matter what race, no matter their background, their beliefs, or their way of life, and recognize that they are also a phenomenal creation of God with limitless potential just like you, who deserves every wonderful thing this life has to offer.

Life has a way of making us forget that we are truly all one. It pulls us into comparison, into judgment, into thinking that we are separate when in truth we are deeply connected. We may differ in race, in culture, in where we were raised, and in what we were taught to believe. Our daily practices may not look the same. The words we use to describe God may sound different. Yet beneath all of that, there is a shared experience that connects us all.

We are human beings trying to make sense of this life. We are doing our best to navigate moments of joy and moments of pain. We are searching for meaning, for peace, and for something that feels steady when everything else feels uncertain. We are all reaching, in our own way, for the same thing. The same feeling. The same love.

When that understanding begins to settle in, something inside of you starts to soften in a very real and noticeable way. The urge to judge others slowly loses its grip, and the need to separate yourself based on beliefs, practices, or labels no longer feels as important as it once did. What begins to take its place is a deeper sense of compassion, a clearer understanding of others, and a quiet kind of love that exists without needing approval or permission from anyone.

Within that space, your perspective begins to shift. You start to recognize that the loneliness you may have felt was never as absolute as it seemed, and that the distance you once believed existed between you and God was never truly there. Even in a world that often appears divided on the surface, there is still a deeper connection that runs through all of us, something steady and unifying that exists beyond differences in belief, background, or experience.

It is within that awareness that peace begins to take root in a more lasting way, that love becomes something you naturally extend rather than something you struggle to find, and that your entire way of moving through life begins to change from the inside out.

3

When Belief Becomes Fear

There was a season in my life when my hair salon became more than a beautiful purple palace where people came to change their appearance. It became a quiet intersection of different belief systems, personalities, and spiritual comfort zones. My salon is all purple, rich and warm, and because I love beauty in all forms, I decorated it with large amethyst crystals. Not small decorative pieces tucked away in corners, but beautiful, bold stones that carried presence. There were at least ten or twelve of them, resting intentionally throughout the space. On the reception desk sat a soft purple sound bowl, simple and elegant, something I enjoyed playing gently in the mornings before clients arrived or occasionally during quiet moments in the day.

For me, those objects were never symbols of rebellion, and they were never meant to stand in opposition to my Christian upbringing. I did not see them as a departure from what I was taught, but rather as an extension of what already lived inside of me. They were simply tools that helped create an atmosphere that felt calm, grounded, and harmonious. I was drawn to the way the sound bowl filled the room with a gentle vibration that seemed to settle the energy in the space. The way the amethyst caught the light and reflected soft shades of purple across the walls created a sense of stillness that felt both peaceful and beautiful. There was nothing dark or unsettling about it to me. It felt balanced. It felt comforting. It felt like peace.

At the same time, I quickly realized that not everyone experienced it in the same way. Some of my clients were deeply rooted in traditional Christian beliefs, the kind of faith that was shaped by strict doctrine and a very clear understanding of what was considered acceptable and what was not. Many of them were women who had grown up in the church just as I had, and I respected that because I understood it. One woman in particular stood out to me. She loved the King James Bible and held tightly to the teachings she had been raised on. She would describe herself as sanctified and filled with the Holy Ghost, and there was a sincerity in her faith that I genuinely admired.

Whenever she walked past the sound bowl, her entire body language would shift in a way that was hard to miss. There was a visible stiffness, a hesitation that showed up before she even said a word. Out of curiosity, I gently struck the bowl one day, allowing the tone to move softly through the room. She immediately reacted with a nervous laugh and said, "Oh my God, let me get out of here before that devil music seeps into my soul." Her tone carried humor, but underneath it, there was a real sense of concern that could not be ignored.

Hearing her say that stayed with me, not because I felt

offended, but because I was genuinely surprised by how differently we were experiencing the exact same thing. The idea that something so simple, a single resonating tone with no words, no hidden meaning, and no intention beyond creating calm, could be perceived as something harmful was difficult for me to understand in that moment. It made me pause and reflect on how much of our perception is shaped by what we have been taught and what we have been told to believe.

I could have argued with her. I could have challenged her directly and asked for proof. I could have tried to educate her on frequency, vibration, and the science behind sound therapy. But in that moment, I realized something important. Forcing my understanding onto her would make me no different than what I sometimes saw others do to prove their point. So instead of reacting defensively, I chose restraint. I simply smiled and walked her to the door. I let her have her perspective without trying to win a debate at the end of a hair appointment. Still, internally, I wrestled with the assumption, but she is not the only one that thinks that way.

It fascinated me how quickly something could be labeled evil simply because it did not look like the worship environment someone was accustomed to. She had no evidence that sound bowls were demonic. There was no scripture she could point to that specifically condemned a resonating tone. Yet the unfamiliarity alone was enough to create suspicion. That moment taught me how deeply fear can shape belief. When we do not understand something, we often assign it a threat level that exceeds reality.

What struck me most was this: the same people who would sit in church and feel the vibration of a powerful organ shaking the walls would call a single calming tone from a bowl dangerous.

Both are beautiful sound. Both are intense vibration. They both move through the air and through the body. The difference is context. One is associated with what feels safe and holy because it is familiar. The other feels foreign and therefore suspect.

That experience in my salon became a quiet lesson in humility for me. It would have been easy to dismiss her as ignorant or narrow minded. I could have rolled my eyes and laugh about her comment. But I had to remember that she believed she was protecting her soul. Her reaction did not come from cruelty. It came from conviction shaped by years of religious doctrine that warned her against anything outside her spiritual framework.

At the same time, I could not ignore how quickly spiritual language is sometimes used to condemn what has not been studied or understood. It is one thing to disagree with a practice. It is another thing to label it as evil without evidence. That pattern has repeated itself throughout history. Anything new, different, or culturally unfamiliar has often been branded as dangerous before being examined.

In that salon, with purple walls and amethyst crystals catching the light, I learned something I carry with me now. Bridging the gap between religion and spirituality is not about proving who is right. It is about understanding where fear is influencing a persons perception. It is about recognizing that sometimes people reject a practice not because it is harmful, but because it feels unfamiliar.

I also learned to check myself. It would be hypocritical for me to criticize someone for labeling my sound bowl as wrong while I silently labeled her rigid or extreme. Division works both ways. Let people be and believe what they choose. Superiority can exist on either side of the conversation. If I truly believe that we are all created by one divine source, then I have to allow space for people to process their beliefs at their own pace.

Over time, I noticed something else. Even the clients who were skeptical still returned. They still sat in the purple room. They still relaxed in the chair. The sound bowl never harmed anyone. The crystals never possessed anyone. The only real tension existed in perception, not in reality. And that realization became powerful for me. It showed me that sometimes the line between religion and spirituality is not built on substance, but on assumption.

That experience deepened my compassion. It reminded me that many people were taught that anything outside their tradition is automatically a threat. When you grow up hearing that certain objects, sounds, or practices are gateways to darkness, that belief can settle deeply into your nervous system. It takes time and safety to question it.

So instead of turning my salon into a battleground of belief, I allowed it to remain what it was meant to be: a peaceful space. I did not hide my crystals. I did not stop playing the bowl. But I also did not force anyone to embrace what made them uncomfortable. I learned that coexistence does not require agreement. It requires maturity.

That small, almost humorous moment about "devil music" revealed something much larger about the human condition. We are quick to defend what we know. We are quick to distrust what we do not. But if we slow down long enough to examine our reactions, we might discover that many of our spiritual fears are inherited rather than investigated.

If we are willing to investigate with humility, we might find that the divine was never threatened by a sound in the first place.

What I began to understand more clearly is that belief

is deeply personal. A person who sincerely believes in a doctrine, whether it is rooted in religion, spirituality, science, or philosophy, is operating within the framework of their own reality. You cannot argue someone out of what they genuinely experience as truth. Their nervous system, their upbringing, their culture, and their personal encounters have shaped that belief. Trying to force someone to see the world through your lens only creates resistance. Peace begins when you release the need to convert every disagreement into a correction.

There is a certain freedom that comes when you allow people to believe what they believe without feeling personally threatened by it. Not every belief must be adopted, and not every practice must be understood, but not every difference must be fought either. If someone's way of connecting with the divine brings them comfort, discipline, hope, or clarity, and it does not harm others, then it is not your responsibility to dismantle it. Maturity is recognizing the difference between a harmful ideology and a harmless preference.

The reality is that belief shapes experience. If a person truly believes that a particular ritual protects them, their body will respond with a sense of safety. If someone believes that a specific prayer brings them closer to God, their heart will open in response to that faith. Belief is powerful, and it is not easily extracted through argument. When we understand that, we stop exhausting ourselves trying to police one another's spiritual lives.

Great peace comes when you allow people to simply be. When you stop scanning for what is different and start observing what is shared, tension dissolves. You no longer feel obligated to debate every symbol, every tradition, every choice. Instead, you measure by impact. Is anyone being harmed? Is someone being manipulated, abused, or oppressed? Is the belief encouraging violence, cruelty, or self destruction? If the answer is no, then perhaps the wisest choice is to step back and allow autonomy.

There is a difference between discernment and interference. Discernment protects against harm. Interference attempts to control what is not ours to control. As long as a person's practice is not illegal, not exploitative, not violent, and not causing pain to themselves or others, it deserves the space to exist. Unity does not require uniformity. It requires restraint, humility, and a willingness to let diversity breathe.

When I embraced that truth, I felt lighter and I stopped feeling responsible for defending every spiritual tool I valued. I no longer allowed myself to feel irritated by every criticism. I stopped interpreting discomfort as attack. Instead, I allowed difference to exist without tension. In doing so, I found something I had been searching for all along: calm.

There is profound serenity in allowing people to walk their path without obstruction. The divine does not need human enforcers. It does not require us to patrol one another's spiritual vocabulary. What it asks, if anything, is that we treat one another with dignity. And dignity includes allowing someone the freedom to believe sincerely in what brings them closer to their understanding of truth. When we stop trying to control belief, we make room for peace, and peace, ultimately, is what most of us are searching for in the first place.

HOLY
BIBLE

4

Tradition, Tools, and the Fear of Losing Control

There is something powerful about tradition. It holds memory. It carries the voices of ancestors. It provides structure when life feels chaotic. When you grow up inside a religious tradition, it becomes more than a belief system. It becomes identity. It shapes how you interpret right and wrong. It influences how you respond to hardship. It even defines how you understand God. Because of that, any practice that exists outside of that framework can feel like a threat, even if the threat is imagined.

As I reflected on the moments in my salon with the amethyst crystals and the sound bowl, I realized that what unsettled some of my clients was not the object itself. It was the possibility that something outside their spiritual training could carry power or meaning. For many people raised in strict religious environments, spiritual authority is centralized. It lives in scripture, in pastors, in churches, in defined rituals. When a tool appears that is not sanctioned by that system, it can feel destabilizing. Not because it is inherently harmful, but because it operates outside familiar control.

Control is an uncomfortable word in spiritual conversations, but it is often present. Structure provides safety. Doctrine provides clarity. Ritual provides repetition that reassures the mind. There is nothing wrong with those things. In fact, they are often beautiful and grounding. But when control becomes rigid, curiosity begins to feel dangerous. If a person has been taught that truth exists only within a specific boundary, anything beyond that boundary can feel like betrayal.

I had to examine this dynamic honestly, not only in others but in myself. It would be easy to point out how quickly someone labeled a sound bowl as demonic. It would be harder to admit that I, too, have felt skeptical of practices I did not immediately understand. Every human being filters new information through their existing beliefs. The difference lies in whether we allow that filter to become a wall.

What I learned through these interactions is that religion often emphasizes protection of doctrine, while spirituality often emphasizes exploration of experience. One protects what has been established. The other experiments with what can be discovered. Both impulses come from somewhere understandable. Protecting tradition can preserve wisdom. Exploring experience can deepen understanding. The tension arises when either side assumes that the other is automatically wrong.

There is also an emotional layer that rarely gets discussed openly. For some people, religion is not only about faith. It is about loyalty. It is about honoring parents, grandparents, and communities who sacrificed and endured while holding onto their beliefs. When someone introduces practices that look unfamiliar, it can feel like dishonoring those who came before. That reaction is deeply emotional, even if it is expressed in doctrinal language.

I think about my grandmother often when I consider these conversations. Her faith was steady and rooted in scripture. She did not burn sage or strike sound bowls. She prayed. She sang. She read her Bible. But what defined her spirituality was not the absence of other tools. It was the presence of love. She did not weaponize her belief. She did not use God as a tool to control others. She trusted what she knew, and she allowed others to walk their path without aggression. That example matters to me because it shows that strong faith does not require hostility toward difference.

When people react strongly to practices like crystals or sound healing, I try to see the fear underneath the reaction rather than just the surface words. Fear often disguises itself as certainty. It can sound bold and confident, but beneath it there is usually anxiety about losing stability. If someone has built their entire understanding of God on a specific set of teachings, anything that expands the conversation can feel destabilizing. And destabilization feels unsafe.

At the same time, spirituality without grounding can also drift into ego. Exploration can become self indulgence if it is not anchored in humility. That is why this conversation is not about replacing religion with spirituality. It is about recognizing that tools are not the source of power. They are methods of engagement. A Bible is paper and ink until someone reads it with sincerity. An amethyst is stone and mineral until someone assigns meaning to it. The object itself is neutral. The intention is what shapes the experience.

When I allowed myself to see that clearly, I stopped feeling defensive in my own space. I did not need to convince anyone that my crystals were holy. I did not need to argue that vibration is scientifically measurable. I simply needed to remain grounded in my own understanding while respecting that others might not be ready to expand theirs. Growth cannot be forced. It unfolds when a person feels safe enough to question their assumptions.

The more I reflect on these experiences, the more I realize that the true conflict between religion and spirituality is rarely about God. It is about comfort zones. It is about how much uncertainty a person can tolerate. It is about whether faith is strong enough to coexist with curiosity. If we believe that the divine source is infinite, then our understanding of that source will always be partial. That realization should make us humble rather than defensive.

In the end, the goal is not to dismantle tradition or glorify experimentation. The goal is maturity. Maturity allows a person to stand firmly in their belief without feeling threatened by someone else's practice. Maturity recognizes that God does not shrink simply because someone strikes a bowl or holds a crystal. And maturity acknowledges that tradition can be honored without condemning everything outside its walls.

As I continue navigating these conversations in my salon and in my life, I remind myself that love is still the measure. If a belief system produces kindness, integrity, and compassion, it carries something sacred. If a practice encourages self awareness and gentleness toward others, it carries something sacred. The form may vary. The posture may vary. But the fruit reveals the alignment.

And when we are brave enough to release the fear of losing control, we might discover that the divine was never confined to our boundaries in the first place.

5

When Ego Wears Spiritual Clothing

Grief can make you reach for anything that promises relief. When my grandmother was murdered in front of me at seventeen years old, something inside me fractured in a way I did not yet have language for. Watching her die from a single gunshot wound to the head at the hands of my grandfather, her husband of thirty two years, altered my nervous system, my understanding of safety, and my sense of reality. Trauma does not politely introduce itself and then fade away. It lingers. It replays. It reshapes how you move through the world. For years, I carried that memory inside my body without truly knowing how to release it.

When you are carrying that kind of pain, healing becomes urgent. It stops being a luxury and starts feeling like survival. By the time I found myself in a spiritual center searching for answers, I was not curious for entertainment. I was desperate. I wanted peace. I wanted the images to stop haunting me. I wanted the heaviness in my chest to dissolve. I wanted to believe that someone, somewhere, had a method that could finally set me free.

That is when I met a man who presented himself as spiritually evolved. He referred to himself as D Amen, or Di Amen De Mere, and he spoke with the authority of someone who believed he had transcended ordinary human limitations. He claimed he had ascended to higher levels of consciousness and self mastery. He positioned himself as a guide who could take others to the same place. When I told him about my grandmother's murder and the trauma I still carried, he assured me that he possessed the knowledge to heal me mentally, emotionally, and spiritually. He told me that through his meditative techniques we would travel back to the day of her death and change the outcome in my subconscious, allowing me to finally release the pain.

When you are broken and someone speaks with certainty about your healing, it can feel like divine intervention. I believed him. I believed that perhaps God had sent this man to help me close a chapter that had defined so much of my life. He told me that our spirits were connected across multiple lifetimes. He said we were twin flames destined to reunite. He said that our meeting was not accidental but spiritually orchestrated. Those words felt profound at the time. They felt purposeful. They felt like confirmation that my suffering had led me exactly where I needed to be.

What I did not recognize then was how easily ego can disguise itself as enlightenment.

As our sessions continued, the boundaries between teacher and student blurred. We read together. We meditated together. He integrated me into parts of his daily life, even bringing me along when he trained clients in his physical fitness work. When our relationship became sexual, I did not resist it because he framed it as a natural extension of our spiritual bond. He told me that due to our deep connection across incarnations, physical intimacy was simply the next stage of alignment. There was no suspicion in me. There was only trust. I believed that this was sacred, not manipulative.

Looking back, I can see how vulnerable I was. I had not yet fully understood my own power. I was still searching for someone outside of me to fix what hurt inside of me. I gave him authority over my healing because I believed he had already achieved the level of spiritual evolution I was striving toward. He spoke of transcending human emotion as though sadness, anger, and fear were weaknesses rather than natural responses to trauma. In his teachings, students were discouraged from expressing pain because he believed that true evolution required rising above emotional attachment.

At first, that philosophy felt empowering. I wanted to transcend my pain. I wanted to rise above it. I thought that if I could detach from my grief, I would finally be free. But as weeks passed, something inside me began to feel disoriented. Suppressing emotion did not make it disappear. It made it resurface in other ways. I found myself sadder, more confused, and less grounded than before. I began to notice that while he spoke about enlightenment, his actions did not reflect humility or integrity.

He lived with a woman he claimed he no longer desired. He told me she was not spiritually aligned with him and that he had made a mistake allowing her to move from another state to be with him. He assured me he was meditating on the divine way to end that relationship while continuing a physical relationship with me. At the time, I accepted his explanations because I believed he was operating from a higher spiritual understanding. In reality, I was ignoring obvious contradictions because my desire for healing was stronger than my instinct for self protection.

Ego is not confined to churches. It is not confined to pulpits. It does not disappear simply because someone replaces scripture with ancient texts or uses words like ascension and consciousness. Ego can exist anywhere a human being believes they are spiritually superior. It can hide behind robes or behind crystals. It can preach doctrine or speak about energy. The form changes. The danger remains the same.

Eventually, his behavior violated the rules of the spiritual center where we met. He was suspended for becoming personally involved with a student. The organization itself did not condone what happened. They took action. But I was left to untangle the emotional aftermath. I had to confront the reality that I had given another human being control over my healing. I had placed my faith in his promises instead of recognizing that the power to heal had always been within me.

That was a painful lesson, but it was transformative.

It forced me to acknowledge that no teacher, preacher, coach, or spiritual guide can do the inner work for you. There may be people who offer tools. There may be people who offer insight. But surrendering your discernment to someone because they appear spiritually advanced is dangerous. True spiritual maturity does not demand your dependence. It encourages your empowerment.

I no longer view that chapter of my life with shame. I view it with understanding. Trauma makes you susceptible to certainty. Grief makes you cling to hope wherever you find it. I take responsibility for my choices, but I also extend compassion to the version of myself who was simply trying to survive unbearable pain.

What that experience ultimately taught me is this: if someone claims to have transcended human emotion yet lacks kindness, humility, and integrity, something is misaligned. If someone insists they hold the key to your healing, be cautious. Healing is not handed to you by another person. It is cultivated within you. God does not outsource your power.

Since then, my spiritual practice has become quieter and more inward. I began sitting in longer periods of meditation not to escape emotion, but to understand it. I allowed myself to feel grief instead of suppressing it. I examined my patterns of self sabotage. I learned that growth does not come from denying your humanity. It comes from integrating it.

Both churches and spiritual centers can contain beautiful guidance. Both can also contain flawed human beings. That reality does not invalidate faith. It simply reminds us to keep our discernment intact. The divine source may work through people, but it does not require you to abandon your intuition.

The ego can wear religious clothing. It can also wear spiritual language. That is why your relationship with God must ultimately be personal. It must be rooted in your own awareness, your own responsibility, and your own willingness to look inward. No one else can walk that path for you.

And once I understood that, I stopped searching for a savior in human form. I realized the tools for my healing had been placed inside me from the beginning.

6

Discernment Is Spiritual Maturity

One of the most difficult lessons I have learned on my journey is that sincerity does not automatically equal integrity. A person can speak passionately about God, about enlightenment, about scripture, about ascension, about divine calling, and still operate from unresolved ego. Titles do not protect us from manipulation. Robes do not guarantee purity. Spiritual vocabulary does not eliminate selfish intent. That realization can be uncomfortable, especially when you genuinely want to believe in the goodness of people who claim to represent something sacred.

After my experience with the spiritual teacher who abused his position, I found myself reflecting not only on what happened to me, but on the broader pattern that exists across religious and spiritual institutions alike. Churches have faced scandals involving pastors and priests who violated trust. Spiritual centers have faced leaders who misuse authority under the guise of higher consciousness. The environments may look different, but the vulnerability of seekers remains the same. Whenever human beings gather around belief, power is present. And wherever power exists, discernment becomes essential.

There is a dangerous misconception that questioning a spiritual leader is equivalent to questioning God. That mindset can silence intuition. It can cause people to ignore red flags because they fear appearing rebellious or faithless. I have seen this dynamic in traditional religious settings where congregants hesitate to challenge authority even when behavior feels wrong. I have also seen it in spiritual communities where teachers are treated as enlightened beings whose words are not to be doubted. In both cases, the common thread is misplaced trust.

Discernment is not cynicism. It is not suspicion for the sake of being guarded. It is awareness rooted in self respect. It is the ability to observe behavior and measure it against truth without surrendering your voice. Healthy spiritual leadership encourages growth and empowerment. Unhealthy leadership demands dependence. That distinction matters more than the label attached to the institution.

Looking back at my own vulnerability, I recognize that grief clouded my discernment. I wanted relief so badly that I ignored inconsistencies. When someone promises to remove your pain completely, it is tempting to overlook contradictions in their character. When someone speaks confidently about higher realms of consciousness, it can feel intimidating to question them. But true spiritual advancement does not diminish your humanity. It does not require you to suppress emotion. It does not isolate you from your own judgment. It strengthens your capacity to think clearly while remaining compassionate.

Discernment also requires self examination. It is easy to point outward and identify flaws in leaders. It is more challenging to ask why we were drawn to them in the first place. Pain seeks comfort. Trauma seeks certainty. Loneliness seeks connection. Those human needs are not weaknesses, but when they go unacknowledged, they can lead us into environments where we hand over our agency. Recognizing that pattern in myself was not an act of shame. It was an act of growth.

There is a sacred balance between guidance and autonomy. Teachers can offer insight. Pastors can interpret scripture. Mentors can share experience. But none of them replace your relationship with God. When guidance becomes control, something has shifted out of alignment. When a leader discourages independent thought or emotional expression, something is wrong. When you feel smaller instead of stronger in someone's presence, your intuition is communicating.

In both religious institutes and spiritual centers, humility should be visible. A true leader understands that they are human. They acknowledge their limitations. They do not claim divine perfection. They do not insist on spiritual superiority. They do not manipulate vulnerability for personal gain. The more someone emphasizes their elevated status, the more cautious we should become. Spiritual maturity often reveals itself through gentleness, not grandiosity.

It took time for me to rebuild trust in my own inner voice after that experience. I had to learn that questioning someone does not mean disrespecting God. I had to understand that discernment is not a lack of faith. It is a component of faith. If we believe that we are created in the image of a divine source, then we possess intuition for a reason. We possess reasoning for a reason. We possess emotional awareness for a reason. Ignoring those gifts in the name of obedience is not spiritual growth. It is self abandonment.

Discernment also protects us from swinging too far in the opposite direction. Pain can sometimes make people reject all institutions entirely. After being hurt by a spiritual leader, it would have been easy for me to declare that all spiritual centers are corrupt. After witnessing scandals in churches, some people conclude that religion itself is flawed beyond redemption. But absolutes rarely reflect reality. There are sincere leaders in churches. There are sincere teachers in spiritual communities. The presence of ego in some does not erase the integrity of others.

What matters is how we approach our own journey. Instead of searching for someone to carry us, we learn to walk with guidance while keeping our footing. Instead of idolizing human beings, we respect their humanity. Instead of outsourcing our healing, we participate actively in it. Discernment allows us to remain open without being naive, compassionate without being exploited, faithful without being blind.

The intersection of religion and spirituality demands maturity because it challenges comfort zones. It invites us to examine both structure and experience through a lens of wisdom. It asks us to honor tradition while thinking independently. It encourages us to explore without losing grounding. None of that is possible without discernment.

I no longer look for someone to elevate me above human emotion. I look for spaces that allow authenticity. I no longer assume that charisma equals credibility. I look for consistency between words and actions. I no longer believe that enlightenment erases humility. I believe that genuine spiritual growth deepens humility.

Discernment is not a barrier to love. It is protection for it.

When we cultivate it, we become less likely to be manipulated by ego dressed in spiritual language. We become less reactive to fear based teachings. We become more stable in our connection to the divine source that does not require intermediaries to validate our worth.

It is in that stability, we find something powerful. We find freedom.

7

The Healing Power of Sound

Sound has always been sacred. Long before debates about religion and spirituality became cultural talking points, human beings were using sound to move emotion, to call on God, to grieve, to celebrate, to unite. The human body responds to vibration whether we acknowledge it or not. A mother hums to soothe her child. A congregation sings to lift its spirit. A drumbeat gathers people into rhythm. Even silence has a frequency that affects the nervous system. When we reduce certain sounds to holy and others to suspicious, we often forget that all sound is vibration traveling through space and through flesh.

In church, I grew up loving the swell of the organ and the power of a choir harmonizing in unity. There is something about gospel music that enters the chest and expands it. When the drums build and the voices rise, it feels like the room is breathing together. That kind of collective worship can shift your emotional state in minutes. It can lift heaviness. It can stir hope. It can make you feel seen in your struggle and strengthened in your faith. No one questions the legitimacy of that kind of sound because it is familiar within religious settings. It is expected. It is sanctioned.

But when someone strikes a sound bowl or allows a tuning fork to hum softly in the air, the reaction can be different. For some people, it feels foreign, almost suspicious. Yet the physical reality is the same. A tone vibrates. The air moves. The body receives it. The nervous system responds. Whether it is a choir filling a sanctuary or a single pure frequency resonating in a quiet room, the body does not distinguish between sacred and secular. It responds to vibration.

In January of 2026, I underwent surgery to remove a tumor from my head. The tumor had eaten into the incus and malleus bones in my ear. Those tiny bones are responsible for transmitting sound, and knowing that something had grown in that space felt symbolic in ways I could not ignore. I was in the hospital for three days. Recovery was not only physical. It was emotional. When you go through something that invasive, you become acutely aware of how fragile the body is and how deeply connected it is to your spiritual state.

Gospel music has always been part of my daily life. I play it every morning when I wake up. It grounds me. It reminds me of my grandmother. It reconnects me to my foundation. But when I came out of surgery, something inside me wanted a different kind of sound. I did not crave the swelling of a choir or the rhythm of drums. I wanted a pure tone. I wanted crown chakra frequencies. I wanted a sustained vibration that felt clean and uninterrupted. When I played those tones, they resonated through my head and into my body in a way that felt restorative.

There was no conflict in that choice. It did not mean I had abandoned gospel. It did not mean I had replaced my faith with something else. It simply meant that in that specific moment, my body responded to a different frequency. Healing is not always linear. Sometimes it requires intensity and praise. Sometimes it requires stillness and subtle vibration. The wisdom is in listening to what your body and spirit need.

That experience deepened my understanding of integration. The organ in a church and the sound bowl in a meditation room are not enemies. Both create resonance. Both shift emotional states. Both can elevate the mind. When a choir sings in harmony, it raises vibration in a collective way. When a tuning fork hums, it raises vibration in a focused way. The mechanism may differ, but the principle is the same. Sound influences energy.

If the choir at your church fills you with hope and motivates you to be kinder, more generous, more patient, then that sound is serving you. If the gentle hum of a tuning fork calms your anxiety and helps you release tension, that sound is serving you. If silence allows you to hear your own thoughts clearly and reconnect with God internally, that too is serving you. There is room for all of it.

The idea that we must choose one and reject the other is another form of unnecessary division. Human beings are complex. Our needs shift. Our seasons change. There may be times in your life when you need the energy of community worship, where drums and voices carry you through pain you cannot lift alone. There may be other times when you need solitude and a single steady tone to help regulate your breath. Neither invalidates the other.

When people speak about raising their vibration, the language can sound abstract, but the concept is practical. When you feel heavy, bitter, or consumed by fear, your behavior reflects that state. When you feel peaceful, grateful, and connected, your behavior reflects that state as well. Sound can be one of the tools that helps transition from one emotional state to another. It is not magic. It is not mystical in a way that replaces responsibility. It is a stimulus that interacts with your nervous system and your mind.

After my surgery, I became even more aware of how intentional I wanted to be with what I allowed into my ears. The ear is not just an organ for hearing. It is a gateway for vibration. It influences balance. It influences perception. The fact that my tumor had affected the bones responsible for transmitting sound felt like a reminder that sound matters more than we often acknowledge. What we listen to shapes us.

This chapter is not about proving that sound bowls are superior to gospel music or that church choirs are superior to meditation tones. It is about acknowledging that both have power. It is about recognizing that God is not confined to one frequency. If a hymn brings you to tears in the best way, lean into it. If a pure tone helps you breathe through recovery, lean into that. The goal is not allegiance to a method. The goal is alignment with love and healing.

We do not have to choose between what nurtures us spiritually and what nurtures us energetically. They are not separate categories. They intersect in the body, in the mind, and in the soul. The more we allow ourselves to experience that without fear, the more integrated our spiritual lives become.

Sound has always been sacred. Whether it echoes through cathedral walls or vibrates softly in a quiet room, it carries the potential to shift us. And if it helps you become more compassionate toward yourself and others, then it has served its purpose.

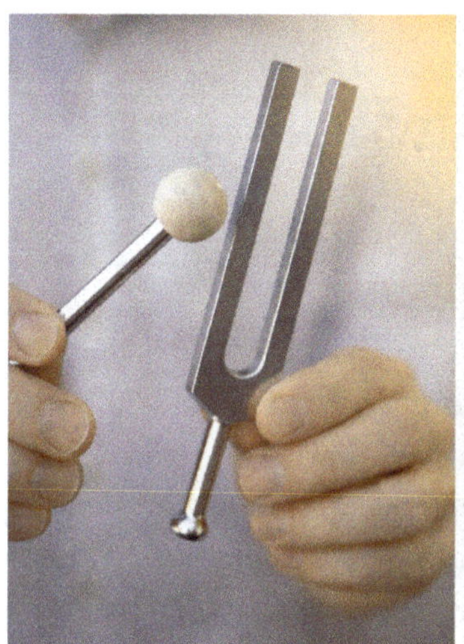

8

The Breath We Share

Breath is so constant that we forget how sacred it is. It is the first thing we do when we enter this world and the last thing we release when we leave it, yet most of us move through our days barely aware of it. We rush. We tighten. We hold our breath without realizing it, as if bracing ourselves against life instead of participating in it. In a world that debates religion and spirituality, argues over doctrine, and separates sacred practices into categories, breath remains untouched by division. No one has to agree on theology to inhale. No one has to convert to exhale.

Breath is not just air moving in and out of the lungs. It is life force. Across cultures and traditions, it has always been understood as more than a physical process. In Christianity, God breathes life into Adam. In Hebrew, the word for spirit and breath share the same root. In Eastern traditions, it is called prana, the vital energy that animates all living beings. In Greek philosophy, pneuma carries similar meaning. Different words, same truth. Breath is the bridge between the body and the unseen. It is where religion and spirituality quietly agree without needing to announce it.

What makes breath so powerful is its honesty. You cannot fake it. Your breath reflects exactly what is happening inside you. When you are anxious, it becomes shallow. When you are afraid, it tightens. When you feel safe, it deepens naturally. Long before the mind explains anything, the breath tells the truth. It does not care what label you claim. It does not care whether you attend church or meditate daily. It responds to your internal state without bias.

Most of us were never taught how to breathe consciously. We were taught how to pray, how to recite scripture, how to meditate, how to think positively, how to behave appropriately. But rarely were we taught how to return to ourselves through the simplest act of all. Conscious breathing is not mystical. It is not reserved for yogis or monks. It is the most accessible spiritual practice available because it does not require belief to function. It requires attention.

When you slow your breath, your nervous system listens. Science confirms what ancient traditions practiced intuitively. Deep diaphragmatic breathing stimulates the vagus nerve, which regulates the body's stress response. It lowers cortisol levels, stabilizes heart rate, and signals to the brain that it is safe to move out of fight or flight. In trauma recovery, therapists often begin not with complex analysis, but with breath regulation. In worship services, when a congregation sings slowly together, their breathing synchronizes. In meditation halls, when silence deepens, breathing steadies. The body does not differentiate between religious and spiritual contexts. It responds to rhythm and safety.

When the breath deepens, the body receives the message that it is safe enough to soften. This is why breath work can feel emotional at times. It touches places words cannot reach. It releases what has been held without demanding explanation. You may find tears rising without a clear story attached. That is not weakness. That is stored tension finding an exit.

Prana is not something you have to summon. Spirit is not something you have to beg for. The breath you are already taking is evidence that life is flowing through you. Breath work does not create life force. It reveals it. It clears pathways that have been constricted by stress, grief, or fear. When breath flows freely, clarity often follows. Calm begins to replace reactivity. The mind becomes less defensive. In that space, compassion becomes easier.

There is nothing extreme about this practice. You do not need incense, a church pew, a yoga mat, or a special posture. Even a few intentional breaths can shift your internal climate. You can feel it almost immediately. The shoulders lower. The jaw releases. The thoughts slow. This is not coincidence. It is design. The same God people pray to on Sundays engineered the nervous system that responds to oxygen and rhythm. The same divine source spiritual seekers meditate toward structured the lungs to expand and contract in perfect intelligence.

Breath is one of the most respectful tools available to us because it never overrides your will. It does not demand allegiance. It meets you where you are. On days when your faith feels strong, breath carries your prayers. On days when your faith feels uncertain, breath carries you anyway. It does not require certainty to function. It supports you whether you call it prayer, meditation, or simply breathing.

What I love most about breath is how inclusive it is. It does not belong to a church, a temple, a mosque, or a spiritual center. It is shared by every living being. Every sermon ever preached traveled on breath. Every chant, every hymn, every sacred text read aloud was carried on breath. Even silent meditation depends on breath as its anchor. Long before humans argued about how to approach God, breath was already connecting them to life.

In a book about religion and spirituality intersecting, breath becomes the simplest proof that sacred does not mean separate. The same oxygen fills the lungs of the pastor and the shaman. The same rhythmic inhale sustains the skeptic and the devotee. The same life force moves through the person who kneels in prayer and the one who sits in meditation. Breath does not discriminate. It does not divide.

The world is ready to remember that breath is not something to rush past. It is something to honor. When you learn to breathe with awareness, you begin to live with awareness. You become less reactive in conversations about belief. You pause before responding. You notice when your chest tightens in defensiveness. You soften before speaking. In that simple pause, division loses momentum.

Returning to breath is returning to common ground. It is a practice that requires no conversion and no argument. It reminds us that beneath doctrine and philosophy, we are biological beings sustained by the same invisible exchange. When you inhale deeply and exhale slowly, you are participating in a rhythm older than any religious institution and wider than any spiritual movement.

There is no hurry here. Healing does not demand urgency. It unfolds when we allow ourselves to slow down and listen. Breath is always available as a meeting place between body and spirit, between religion and spirituality, between you and the divine source that animates everything.

Perhaps if we learned to breathe together more often, we would argue less and understand more.

9

Living Sacred Without Fear

Living Sacred Without Fear

The Science of Sound and the Power of Belief

There has been increasing research over the past several decades on the impact of sound on the human nervous system. While ancient cultures intuitively understood the role of vibration in healing, modern neuroscience and psychology have begun to document what many traditions already practiced. Studies in sound therapy, music therapy, and frequency based interventions show measurable reductions in stress hormones such as cortisol, improvements in heart rate variability, and shifts in brainwave patterns from high stress beta states into calmer alpha and theta states. Psychiatrists and psychologists who use music therapy in clinical settings have documented its effectiveness in reducing anxiety, improving mood disorders, and supporting trauma recovery. Hospitals use calming frequencies in certain post operative recovery environments because sound influences physiological regulation.

When it comes to meditation tones, tuning forks, or singing bowls, research shows that sustained harmonic frequencies can stimulate the vagus nerve, which plays a central role in emotional regulation and the body's rest and repair state. Functional MRI studies have shown that specific auditory frequencies can shift neural activity in areas associated with emotional processing. The science is still evolving, but what is clear is that vibration affects the body.

What is interesting is that many of the same measurable benefits are observed in communal religious music settings. Choir singing has been studied extensively, and researchers have found that group singing increases oxytocin, the hormone associated with bonding and trust. Congregational singing has been shown to synchronize heart rates among participants, creating physiological coherence in a shared space. Drumming circles, often used in both spiritual and church contexts, have been shown to reduce stress and increase feelings of connection. Organ music, with its deep resonant frequencies, activates similar neurological pathways as meditation tones. The difference is not in the biology. The difference is in the interpretation.

When someone says that sound bowls are beneficial but church music is not scientific, they are overlooking research that validates both. When someone says that only worship music is holy and sound healing is demonic, they are ignoring the physiological reality that both are forms of vibration interacting with the nervous system. The body does not argue theology. It responds to frequency.

The deeper question then becomes not whether sound works, but how belief shapes the experience of sound. Placebo research has shown repeatedly that expectation influences outcome.

When a person believes something will help them, the brain releases chemicals that support that belief. That does not mean the effect is imaginary. It means the mind and body are interconnected. If someone believes that wearing a cross protects them, that belief can generate a sense of safety that reduces stress. If someone believes that wearing amethyst protects them from negative energy, that belief can create the same physiological calm. The object is not the only factor. The belief is powerful.

That does not make belief foolish. It makes it human.

Wearing Your Cross and Wearing Your Crystals

There was a time when I would hesitate before wearing crystals in certain environments. I knew the assumptions that might follow. I knew the looks. But I also know what it feels like to wear a cross around my neck and feel connected to my grandmother's faith. I know what it feels like to hold a piece of amethyst and feel grounded. I refuse to accept that one symbol is legitimate while the other is shameful.

It is done unto you as you believe.

That phrase is not about delusion. It is about responsibility. If you believe something is harmful, your nervous system will react as if it is harmful. If you believe something is supportive, your body will respond accordingly. That is not mystical thinking. That is psychological reality. You do not have to adopt someone else's interpretation of an object or a ritual. You do not have to accept their fear as your truth.

There are Christians who choose not to celebrate Halloween because they associate it with ancient pagan practices. They interpret its origins through a lens of spiritual caution. At the same time, millions of families allow their children to dress in costumes and collect candy without any intention of celebrating darkness. The meaning of an action is shaped by intention. If you are not honoring evil, then you are not participating in evil. You do not have to accept someone else's negative narrative for something that, in your lived reality, holds no dark intention.

The same principle applies to crystals. I was skeptical when I first became interested in them. I did not accept their significance blindly. I researched. I watched videos of crystal mining, seeing amethyst, citrine, malachite, and selenite pulled from the earth. I watched miners carefully extract these stones from caves and mountains. These are not artificial inventions. They are natural formations created over time within the earth itself. If we believe that God created the earth, then these stones exist within that creation.

In many countries outside of America, the relationship with the earth is integrated into daily life. When I spent time in Peru with a shaman, I learned how deeply they respect the earth. They referred to it as Pachamama. The earth was not separate from spirituality. It was central to it. Gratitude for the land was part of prayer. Connection to nature was not considered alternative. It was considered foundational.

In America, conversations about spirituality often center around buildings and institutions rather than the natural world. That does not make American faith inferior. It simply reveals cultural emphasis. In Peru, in parts of Asia, in parts of Africa, and in many indigenous communities around the world, spirituality and earth are intertwined. They see God in mountains, rivers, and soil. They do not separate reverence for the Creator from reverence for creation.

If we live on this earth, and this earth provides minerals,

plants, and natural frequencies, then using those elements with gratitude does not automatically contradict faith. It depends on intention. It depends on alignment. It depends on whether those practices are leading you toward humility and love or toward ego and superiority.

Public Integration Without Apology

Living sacred in modern life requires courage because people are quick to categorize. If you wear a cross and attend church, some will assume you reject spirituality. If you wear crystals and meditate, some will assume you reject religion. But human beings are not as binary as social media narratives suggest. You can honor your grandmother's faith and also sit in silence with a tuning fork. You can sing in a choir and also ground your feet in the grass. You do not have to shrink yourself to fit someone else's comfort zone.

The key is discernment and integrity. Ask yourself whether what you are practicing makes you kinder. Ask whether it strengthens your character. Ask whether it draws you closer to humility or inflates your ego. If a practice leads you toward compassion, forgiveness, and responsibility, it is serving your growth. If it leads you toward arrogance, isolation, or superiority, it is time to reassess.

Belief systems become dangerous when they are weaponized. They become powerful when they are internalized responsibly. No one can force you to accept their interpretation of God. No one can assign negative intention to your actions if you are not operating from that intention. You do not have to argue with everyone who disagrees. Sometimes living peacefully is the most powerful statement.

When I reflect on my journey from strict religious upbringing to spiritual exploration and back into integration, I see a pattern of expansion rather than abandonment. I did not lose my foundation. I deepened it. I did not replace church music with sound bowls. I added understanding. I did not discard scripture. I expanded my awareness of creation.

The world does not need more division over labels. It needs more maturity. It needs people who can say, "This works for me," without insisting it must work for everyone else. It needs people who can respect a cross and respect a crystal without feeling threatened.

Ultimately, if God created this earth, then everything within it carries potential. How we use that potential determines whether it elevates or harms us. If the choir raises your vibration and inspires you to serve others, embrace it. If a tuning fork calms your mind after surgery and helps your body heal, embrace it. If both bring you closer to love, there is no conflict.

Sacred does not mean narrow. It means intentional.

And living sacred in modern life means refusing to let fear dictate your expression of faith.

10

One Source, One Responsibility

There comes a point in spiritual growth when the conversation shifts from what other people believe to what you are willing to embody. It is easy to talk about unity. It is easy to say that religion and spirituality intersect. It is easy to critique ego in institutions and point out hypocrisy in leaders. The more difficult work begins when you ask yourself whether your own life reflects the love you claim to believe in. Integration is not philosophical. It is behavioral.

For a long time, I searched outside of myself for certainty. I searched for teachers, for systems, for answers that would finally make everything make sense. I wanted someone to tell me that healing would be permanent and painless. I wanted assurance that if I aligned with the correct practice, the right doctrine, the highest frequency, then I would be immune to confusion and grief. Life does not work that way. The divine does not remove our responsibility simply because we adopt the right language.

What I have learned through church pews, through monasteries in Greece, through spiritual centers, through my salon, through surgery, through betrayal, through grief, is that everything eventually leads back to accountability. You cannot outsource your spiritual maturity. You cannot blame religion for division while harboring resentment in your own heart. You cannot criticize spirituality for ego while refusing to examine your own pride. The intersection of religion and spirituality is not just about merging practices. It is about merging integrity with awareness.

When we say that there is one divine source, that statement carries weight. It means that every human being you encounter is animated by the same breath that animates you. It means that the person singing in a choir and the person meditating on a mountain are sustained by the same life force. If that is true, then the way you treat others becomes the most accurate reflection of your faith. The symbols you wear are secondary. The music you prefer is secondary. The label you claim is secondary. What matters is how you show up.

The world is deeply divided right now. People are quick to categorize and quicker to condemn. Religion is often used as a boundary marker. Spirituality is often used as a badge of independence. In both spaces, I have seen kindness. In both spaces, I have seen cruelty. The difference is never the framework itself. It is the human being operating within it. That realization is both sobering and empowering. It means that the future of unity does not depend on institutions alone. It depends on individuals.

There was a time when I believed that if enough people adopted a more open perspective, division would disappear.

What I understand now is that openness without responsibility is fragile. You can speak about unity and still react defensively when challenged. You can claim to love everyone and still judge quietly in your thoughts. The work is internal before it becomes external. Integration begins in the mind and in the heart long before it appears in public behavior.

When I think about my grandmother, I think about the quiet consistency of her faith. She did not need to debate anyone about doctrine. She did not need to defend her belief aggressively. She lived it. That is the standard I return to. Not perfection. Not superiority. Consistency. If I say that love is the ultimate measure, then love must be visible in my reactions, in my patience, in my forgiveness. It must be visible when someone disagrees with me. It must be visible when someone misinterprets me. Otherwise, my spirituality is only theoretical.

The responsibility of living sacred in modern life is not glamorous. It is daily. It shows up in conversations at family gatherings when topics become tense. It shows up when someone labels your practice as wrong and you choose not to retaliate. It shows up when you witness hypocrisy and decide to respond with clarity instead of bitterness. It shows up when you resist the temptation to become spiritually superior simply because you have experienced both sides.

One of the most powerful realizations I have had is that unity does not require uniformity. We do not need everyone to believe the same thing in order to coexist peacefully. What we need is emotional maturity. We need the ability to recognize that someone else's method of connecting with God does not diminish our own. We need the strength to hold our beliefs without using them as weapons. That kind of maturity is rare because it requires humility.

Humility is not weakness. It is clarity about your limitations. It is understanding that your perspective, no matter how deeply informed, is still partial. No single person sees the entirety of the divine. No single tradition holds the complete expression of truth. When we accept that reality, curiosity becomes possible. Respect becomes possible. Dialogue becomes possible. The moment we insist that our understanding is absolute, growth stops.

There is also a responsibility to protect ourselves. Integration does not mean naivety. Discernment remains essential. Not every spiritual leader operates with integrity. Not every religious authority reflects love. Accountability applies to everyone, including ourselves. The lesson is not to reject all institutions. The lesson is to engage with awareness. Trust should be earned through consistency, not demanded through titles.

As I look back on the journey that brought me here, I see how each experience stripped away a layer of illusion. The illusion that religion and spirituality must compete. The illusion that someone else could heal me completely. The illusion that symbols hold power independent of intention. The illusion that division is inevitable. What remains is something simpler and stronger than any label. What remains is responsibility.

Responsibility for how I interpret what I see. Responsibility for how I respond to what I do not understand. Responsibility for how I use the tools available to me. Responsibility for my healing. Responsibility for my impact on others. If there is truly one source animating us all, then every action either aligns with that source or distances us from it.

There will always be differences in expression. There will always be cultural distinctions, theological disagreements, and varied spiritual practices. Those differences do not have to become fault lines. They can become invitations to expand our understanding of how vast the divine truly is. The choice belongs to us.

When I say one source, one responsibility, I mean that unity begins with personal integrity. It begins with refusing to let fear dictate belief. It begins with acknowledging that love is the only standard that does not contradict itself. If something makes you cruel, it is not aligned. If something makes you kinder, it deserves consideration.

The world does not need more arguments about which path is superior. It needs more people who embody compassion consistently. It needs more people who can sit in church on Sunday and meditate on Monday without feeling conflicted. It needs more people who can wear a cross and a crystal without apology. It needs more people who understand that sacred does not mean separate.

In the end, the intersection of religion and spirituality is not a battlefield. It is a meeting place. It is where structure and experience shake hands. It is where tradition and exploration acknowledge each other. It is where sound and silence both find purpose. It is where grief becomes wisdom. It is where ego is confronted. It is where healing becomes personal responsibility.

You do not have to choose between what shaped you and what expanded you. You do not have to shrink your understanding to fit someone else's comfort. You do not have to defend your peace with aggression. You only have to live in alignment with the love you claim to believe in.

Everything circles back to that.

And when you truly accept that there is one source animating all of us, the division loses its grip. What remains is your daily choice to embody the sacred in a way that honors that truth.

That choice is yours, and it always has been.

11

Stillness Is the Meeting Place

If there is one place where religion and spirituality quietly embrace each other, it is in stillness.

When you strip away the language, the rituals, the symbols, the doctrines, the debates, and the cultural expressions, what remains at the center of both prayer and meditation is the same act. It is the act of becoming still. It is the act of turning inward. It is the act of acknowledging that you are not the highest authority in your own life. Whether you kneel beside a bed or sit cross legged on the floor, whether you fold your hands or rest them on your knees, the posture is secondary to the intention. The intention is connection.

Growing up, I was taught that prayer was conversation with God. You speak. You ask. You confess. You thank. In many Christian environments, prayer carries an element of pleading. There is a tone of proving worthiness, of asking God to forgive, to intervene, to bless, to rescue. There is humility in that posture, and humility is beautiful. Recognizing that we are not self sustaining beings can keep the ego in check. But over time, I began to question whether pleading was the only language available to us.

When I began exploring meditation more deeply, I noticed something different. Meditation did not begin with begging. It began with awareness. It began with remembering that the divine source is already present. It encouraged stillness rather than performance. It encouraged listening rather than convincing. It suggested that worthiness is not earned but remembered. That idea felt both foreign and freeing.

For a while, I felt tension between those two approaches. Was I supposed to humble myself through constant confession and request, or was I supposed to operate from the belief that I was already aligned with divine worth? The more I matured spiritually, the more I realized that these are not opposites. They are different emphases within the same relationship.

Prayer, at its healthiest, is honest conversation. It is not groveling. It is not self humiliation. It is vulnerability. It is bringing your fears, your hopes, your gratitude, and your confusion before the source you believe created you. Meditation, at its healthiest, is receptive awareness. It is quieting the mental noise long enough to sense guidance, peace, or clarity from within. When prayer becomes desperate begging rooted in unworthiness, it can reinforce shame. When meditation becomes ego driven affirmation detached from accountability, it can reinforce pride. But when both are practiced with balance, they meet beautifully.

I no longer see prayer and meditation as separate disciplines. I see them as two directions within the same sacred conversation. Sometimes I speak. Sometimes I listen. Sometimes I express gratitude out loud. Sometimes I sit silently and allow gratitude to rise naturally. Sometimes I ask for strength. Sometimes I remember that strength has already been placed within me.

The idea that humans must constantly prove their worth to God has shaped many religious narratives. At the same time, the spiritual idea that humans are born inherently worthy can feel threatening to those raised in strict doctrines of sin and redemption. But perhaps both are pointing to a deeper truth. Perhaps humility is necessary not because we are worthless, but because we are powerful. Perhaps remembering our inherent worth does not eliminate responsibility, but strengthens it.

If we believe we were created in the image of a divine source that is love, then worth is not something we manufacture. It is something we inherit. That does not mean we avoid growth. It does not mean we ignore mistakes. It means we correct ourselves from a place of dignity rather than shame. Begging for love that is already available keeps us small. Remembering that love while still striving to live responsibly keeps us grounded.

Meditation teaches awareness of thought patterns. It reveals where fear lives. It exposes self sabotage. Prayer invites surrender of those patterns to something greater than the individual ego. Together, they create balance. One builds clarity. The other builds trust. One quiets the mind. The other opens the heart. Neither requires competition.

In modern life, where distraction is constant and opinions are loud, stillness is revolutionary. Choosing to sit quietly, even for a few minutes, disrupts the chaos. Choosing to pray without performance and meditate without superiority shifts the internal climate. It reminds you that the divine source does not require spectacle. It requires sincerity.

When I meditate, I am not rejecting my Christian upbringing.

I am honoring the same God my grandmother prayed to, but I am honoring that presence through silence as well as speech. When I pray, I am not rejecting the lessons I learned from spiritual exploration. I am simply engaging with the divine in a language that shaped my earliest understanding. There is room for both because the source is not fragile.

What matters most is not whether you call it prayer or meditation. What matters is whether it makes you more loving. Does your stillness soften your reactions? Does your conversation with God reduce your fear? Does your awareness increase your compassion? If the answer is yes, then you are aligned.

This book has never been about convincing you to abandon what raised you. It has never been about persuading you to adopt practices that do not resonate. It has been about dissolving unnecessary division. It has been about recognizing that sacred does not mean separate. It has been about understanding that structure and experience can coexist.

You do not have to choose between kneeling and sitting. You do not have to choose between singing and listening. You do not have to choose between wearing a cross or wearing a crystal. You do not have to choose between church and nature. You do not have to beg for worth, and you do not have to inflate yourself with ego. You simply have to return to stillness and remember who you are. There is one source. There is one breath moving through all of us. There is one responsibility to live in alignment with love. Everything else is expression.

When you close this book, I hope you feel lighter. I hope you feel less defensive. I hope you feel permission to exist fully in your complexity. I hope you feel the freedom to honor your grandmother's prayers and your own meditations without apology. I hope you sit in stillness and feel that you are already enough, already loved, already connected.

Sacred. Not separate. One love.

12

Conclusion

One God, One Love

As I bring this book to a close, what sits most heavily on my heart is not doctrine, not debate, not which side anyone chooses, but humanity itself. I have lived long enough, traveled far enough, suffered deeply enough, and healed honestly enough to know that division does not serve us. I have seen what happens when people cling to labels more tightly than they cling to compassion. I have watched conversations dissolve into arguments because someone felt their belief was being threatened. And through all of it, I keep returning to something simple and unshakable: if God is truly love, then anything rooted in cruelty cannot represent Him.

It concerns me how easily people are excluded in the name of righteousness. Entire communities are pushed aside because of race, religion, or sexual orientation as if the divine source that created the universe makes mistakes when creating human beings. I cannot accept that. The God I have come to understand through prayer, through meditation, through church, through travel, and through stillness does not operate from insecurity. There is no need for God to be defended through hate. When belief produces harshness, something has gone off course.

I am not asking anyone to abandon their convictions. Convictions can be beautiful when they are grounded in humility. What I am asking is that we examine what our convictions produce. Do they make us more patient with people who are different? Do they expand our capacity to forgive? Do they increase our empathy? If a belief system makes someone more rigid, more angry, more eager to condemn, then it deserves to be examined honestly. Spiritual maturity is not proven by how loudly someone defends their position. It is revealed in how gently they treat others.

There is one source of life. Whether someone calls that source God, Jehovah, Elohim, the Universe, or Creator does not change the origin. If we truly believe we were created by one divine intelligence, then every human being is carrying something sacred. That includes people whose practices we do not understand. That includes people whose lifestyles do not mirror our own. That includes people whose worship looks unfamiliar. Respecting someone's humanity does not require agreement with every choice they make. It requires recognition that they were not created to be discarded.

Over the years, I have worn a cross and I have worn crystals. I have sung in worship and I have sat in meditation. None of those expressions made me superior, and none of them made me condemned. What shaped my growth was whether I allowed those practices to soften me. When faith makes you kinder to the person in front of you, it is aligned. When spirituality makes you more accountable for your own behavior, it is aligned.

If something encourages you to treat others with dignity, it reflects the divine. If it encourages you to belittle or ostracize, it does not.

World peace is not an abstract dream reserved for governments and global summits. It begins in individual interactions. It begins in how you respond when someone challenges your beliefs. It begins in whether you choose curiosity over defensiveness. It begins in whether you can sit at a table with people who practice differently and still see their humanity. If enough individuals commit to operating from love rather than ego, the collective atmosphere shifts.

I speak from concern because I see how divided we have become. I speak from love because I believe we are capable of better. We do not need more spiritual superiority. We do not need more arguments about who has the correct path. We need more compassion, more self awareness, and more responsibility. We need people who understand that sacred does not mean exclusive. It means worthy of reverence, and humanity itself is worthy of reverence.

The most reliable measure I have found is this: if something makes you cruel to yourself or to someone else, it is not reflecting God. If something strengthens your ability to uplift others, to forgive, to show patience, then it is moving you closer to alignment. The standard is not complicated. Love does not require complex interpretation.

My hope is that when you close this book, you feel free. Free to honor your upbringing without rejecting what you have learned along the way. Free to meditate without feeling disloyal to prayer. Free to pray without feeling unsophisticated. Free to wear your symbols without shame. Free to let other people do the same. There is one God. There is one love. Everything else is expression. Do not allow anyone to tell you that your expression to God is wrong.

If we can hold onto that, truly hold onto it, then acceptance becomes natural rather than forced. And when acceptance becomes natural, peace is no longer an abstract idea. It becomes a daily practice.

That is the world I hope we move toward together. That is how the World as a whole will change for the better.

About the Author

SaBrina Fisher Reece was once known throughout California as "The Braid Queen." For more than twenty-six years, she owned and operated the legendary Braids By SaBrina, a celebrated salon and school on Adams Boulevard in Los Angeles. It grew into the largest and most influential braiding establishment in the city, where artistry, empowerment, discipline, and community came together in powerful ways. Her success was entirely self-made, built through perseverance, resilience, and vision, often without consistent external support or validation.

As she stepped into the second half of her life, SaBrina felt a deeper calling unfolding within her. The story behind her success was not just one of entrepreneurship, but one of faith, healing, self-trust, and spiritual awakening. Early experiences of abandonment and profound personal loss led her inward, where she began the real work of emotional healing and inner mastery. What started as creative expression evolved into purposeful transformation.

Today, SaBrina writes self-help books rooted in emotional healing, personal growth, and spiritual awareness. Blending lived experience with motivational insight and metaphysical understanding, she explores themes of balance, resilience, self-mastery, and the unseen forces that shape human thought and behavior. Through her writing and motivational speaking, she guides readers toward deeper self-awareness, renewed confidence, and lives that feel intentional and aligned from the inside out.

She is the author of numerous self-help and transformational works, including *My Spiritual Smile, Kicking Depression In the Butt, Your Mind Is Magic, Perfectly Positive, Living Life on a Higher Frequency, Spiritual Balance, Angry World, Become Your Own Cheerleader, God is Not a Man: Rediscovering the Divine Balance of Masculine and Feminine Within Us All, Self Sabotage, How to Get Exactly What You Want From God, When I Say "I Am"*, and the popular Ebooks: *Imagine: Learn How to Use Your Imagination to Design the Life You Desire, You're Not Religious -You're Spiritual-I Get It: Bridging the Gap Between the Two, , Take A Breath With Bri: The Power of Intentional Breathing, Is This Why They Burned The Books?: Buried Wisdom From The Past.*

Her passion for sound and frequency has led her to explore the healing power of crystal sound bowls, tuning forks, and flow chimes, tools designed to help harmonize the body, mind, and spirit. Now residing in the enchanting landscapes of New Mexico, "The Land of Enchantment," she offers Sound Vibration Sessions that invite others to slow down, breathe deeply, and reconnect with their higher selves. While she embraces these modalities, she reminds her students and readers that there is no single path to peace. Every journey is sacred, and every sincere method of connecting with the Divine carries value.

Above all, SaBrina is a devoted mother of four, Justin, Joi, Jayden, and Journey, and a proud grandmother to Raiden Jesse and Rio Jordan. Watching them, and those she teaches, awaken to their divine potential remains her greatest joy.

Her message is simple and enduring: we are each born with divine energy, a God-given power to create, to heal, and to live fully. The goal is not perfection, but peace. The journey is not to escape life, but to embrace it, to use positive tools to take control of the mind and become the master of your fate.

You can connect with me on:

https://www.facebook.com/BooksBySaBrinaFisherReece

Also by Bri Reece

Angry World (EBOOK)
Understanding the Root Causes of Anger: This book is for anyone who has ever lost their temper and felt ashamed afterward. I have been there. I know what it feels like to react and then regret it. Be gentle with yourself. Anger does not make you broken. It means something inside you needs healing. You can always learn a better way to respond, to communicate, and to choose peace.

When I Say "I AM"

What you say after "I Am" has the power to shape your entire life.

In *When I Say "I Am"*, SaBrina Fisher Reece reveals the sacred and scientific power of spoken identity. Blending spiritual truth, biblical wisdom, and universal law, this transformational book teaches readers how their words are not just communication—but creation. Every "I Am" statement becomes a command to the subconscious, a signal to the universe, and a declaration to the spiritual realm.

Drawing from scripture, including God's revelation of "I AM" as the eternal source of being, SaBrina shows how the same creative force lives within each of us. Through emotionally moving insight, practical affirmations, and deep spiritual awareness, readers learn how to shift from fear-based language to faith-based declarations that activate healing, confidence, abundance, and purpose.

This book will help you: Break negative identity patterns, Reprogram limiting beliefs, Speak life instead of fear. Align your words with divine promise

Use "I Am" as a daily tool for transformation

More than motivation, *When I Say "I Am"* is a blueprint for conscious creation. It reminds you that your voice is powerful, your identity is sacred, and your words are always working, either for you or against you.

If you are ready to stop speaking survival and start speaking destiny, this book will show you how to command your life with intention, faith, and divine authority, one "I Am" at a time.

Is This Why They Burned The Books? Buried Wisdom from the Past

What if the most powerful knowledge was never destroyed... only buried?

Across history, libraries have burned, philosophers have been silenced, and ancient civilizations have disappeared. Yet fragments of their wisdom continue to surface in unexpected places. In sacred geometry carved into stone. In healing traditions rooted in the earth. In philosophies that challenge us to master the mind. In spiritual teachings that insist the kingdom is within.

In *Is This Why They Burned the Books?*, Bri Reece takes readers on a deeply personal and thought provoking journey through ancient Egypt, Peru, and Greece, exploring the possibility that humanity once understood more about consciousness, energy, and inner power than we acknowledge today.

Drawing from travel experiences inside the Great Pyramid of Giza, meditation above Machu Picchu, and reflections in Delphi and Meteora, this book bridges ancient civilizations with modern self awareness. It asks bold but balanced questions:

What did our ancestors know about the mind?

Why do certain ideas about human potential keep resurfacing across centuries?

Are we operating at only a fraction of our true capacity?

What does evolving to a higher self actually look like?

This is not a conspiracy book. It is a curiosity book. It does not attack religion. It expands perspective. It does not claim certainty. It invites exploration. Through thoughtful reflection on ancient wisdom, energy, grounding, inner discipline, and the vastness of the universe, Bri Reece offers readers something far more valuable than answers. She offers responsibility. The responsibility to think deeply, to seek humbly, and to remember that human potential is far from exhausted.

If you have ever felt that there is more to this life than routine and repetition...

If you are a seeker who questions without arrogance... If you sense that buried wisdom is waiting to be rediscovered...

This book is for you. The fire may have burned the pages. But the wisdom remains.

Second by Second
Daily Tools to Co-Create a Great Life: explores the concept that human beings actively shape their reality through thought, emotion, and intentional focus.

Drawing from spiritual principles, practical psychology, and personal experience, Bri Reece presents a structured approach to conscious co-creation. The book emphasizes the power of visualization, emotional alignment, and disciplined thought management as daily tools for personal transformation.

Through relatable stories and accessible instruction, readers learn how to:

-Recognize and redirect limiting thought patterns
-Use imagination as a creative instrument
-Align emotion with desired outcomes
-Integrate spiritual belief with personal responsibility

Bri Reece presents co-creation as a partnership between the individual and the divine, offering readers a framework for intentional living grounded in faith, awareness, and consistent practice.

This book is designed for readers interested in personal development, spirituality, mindset mastery, and practical tools for self-directed growth.

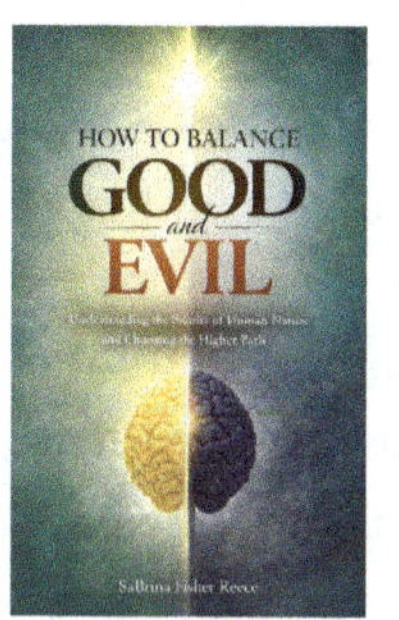

How to Balance Good and Evil Understanding the Polarity of Human Nature and Choosing the Higher Path

What if "good" and "evil" are not distant forces fighting somewhere outside of you-but daily choices happening quietly within you?

In this powerful and deeply personal book, SaBrina Fisher Reece explores the truth about human nature: we are all born into a world of polarity. Light and shadow. Compassion and cruelty. Fear and love. The tension is not proof that you are broken—it is proof that you have been given free will.

This book does not label people as evil. It does not shame anger, frustration, or human imperfection. Instead, it teaches you how to recognize the internal tug-of-war we all experience and how to consciously choose the higher path without denying your humanity.

Through raw personal stories, leadership lessons, parenting moments, business experiences, and spiritual insight, SaBrina reveals how polarity shows up in everyday life-at work, in relationships, in traffic, in conflict, and even in your own thoughts. She demonstrates that self-regulation, compassion, emotional control, and imagination are powerful tools that help you move toward integrity instead of impulse.

You will learn:

How to understand the "dark side" without being ashamed of it

Why emotional control is a life-saving skill

How small daily choices shape your character

The difference between reacting and choosing

How compassion creates a better world without tolerating abuse

Why discipline is required to consistently choose your higher self

This book is for men, women, and young people who want to grow spiritually without judgment or religious condemnation. It is for those who understand that while horrific acts exist in the world, no one is born destined for darkness. We are given a choice every day.

You wake up at the center of the pole.

The direction you lean becomes the person you become.

If you are ready to understand yourself more deeply, lead with your heart, and consciously choose the higher side of who you are, this book will guide you there.

Staying Happy in the Midst of Havoc
How to Hold On to Joy and Peace When the World Is Falling Apart is a heartfelt and empowering guide for navigating life's most uncertain and overwhelming moments. In a world filled with chaos, fear, and unexpected challenges, this book reminds readers that while we cannot control everything happening around us, we can control how we respond.

Through powerful real-life experiences and practical tools, SaBrina Fisher Reece shows how to remain grounded, choose peace, and protect your emotional well-being even in the face of personal crises, global unrest, and everyday struggles. From family emergencies and health scares to the stress of living in unpredictable times, this book offers a steady and reassuring path forward.

With a warm and compassionate voice, this guide helps readers shift their mindset, build resilience, and make happiness a daily, intentional practice. Staying Happy in the Midst of Havoc is for anyone seeking calm, strength, and clarity in a world that often feels out of control.

In Mind Is All

Manipulating Ideas in a New Direction, SaBrina Fisher Reece explores the mechanics of thought-how ideas form, how they gain power, and how they quietly shape decisions, behavior, and belief. This book focuses less on positivity as a concept and more on mental leadership: learning how to consciously guide thought before it guides you.

Rather than motivating through inspiration alone, this book challenges readers to examine where their attention goes and why. It offers a framework for recognizing habitual thinking and deliberately steering it in a new, more constructive direction.

In this book, you'll learn how to:

Identify ideas that limit your growth
Redirect mental momentum instead of fighting it
Strengthen focus and internal discipline
Replace unconscious reactions with intentional thought
Use awareness to influence outcomes and decisions

Mind Is All is about reclaiming authority over your inner world. When you learn how ideas are formed and sustained, you gain the ability to reshape them-and in doing so, reshape your experience of life.

This book is for readers ready to think differently, not just feel better.

www.ingramcontent.com/pod-product-compliance
Lightning Source LLC
La Vergne TN
LVHW010616110826
845149LV00003B/930

9781971622637